Introduction: Veiling and Modesty, Control or Liberation?

Islamic veiling, or hejab, is practiced in many Muslim

cultures, yet its context varies from country to country. In Iran,

under the Islamic regime which has been in power since the 1979

revolution, women are forced to observe hejab in the name of the

Koran. Any infraction results in immediate punishments, yet women

often resist the veil and use it to their advantage. The circumstances

surrounding the resurgence of veiling in Egypt are quite different,

however. Since the early 1980s and despite its abolition which

began in the 1920s, women have been voluntarily taking up the veil.

They often do so in order to be seen as more respectable, to protect

themselves from harassment, and in order to navigate the workplace

environment. Though veiling in the United States is generally

relegated to Muslim communities, a new argument involving

women's clothing is surfacing: a call to modesty which implores

women to alter their dress or take up the veil in order to protect

themselves from sexual harassment and rape. In addition,

fundamentalist Christian communities, specifically the Holdeman

Mennonites, require women to observe a strict, modest dress code.

In all of these cases, veiling or "conservative" dress is seen as a means of protecting women from the unwanted advances of men. However, further exploration reveals that although "modest" dress can provide a means for women to negotiate their environments, it truly is a tool for controlling their behavior and maintaining an environment of hostility and patriarchal privilege.

Iran

Imposition and Enforcement of Hejab

Currently in Iran, women are required by law to wear the veil and observe hejab, the complete covering of a woman. According to Ayatollah Khomeini, "no part of a woman's body may be seen except her face and the part of her hand between her wrist and her fingers" (Tohidi 1991: 253). The government's preferred method of veiling is the use of the chador, an all-enveloping cover which is worn over a scarf on the head. It is made from a single piece of material, and it must be held in place by holding on to its ends and securing it over the head with one's hands (Afshar 1998: 197).

A woman who refuses to comply with hejab is considered to have committed a crime which is punished by either imprisonment for up to a year or seventy-five lashes. If a woman is deemed improperly covered, it is not necessary that she be taken to court. Rather, her crime is "self-evident," and immediately punishable (1991: 319). This practice of veiling is enforced by government appointed officials who are part of "bands of club-wielders" (Tohidi 1991: 253). Sometimes women are physically attacked in the streets with knives and guns by these bands (usually organized by the "Center to Fight the Undesired") and rarely survive. The staunchest supporters and enforcers of these modesty codes are members of the Hezbollahi party (the Party of God, fervent government supporters). In addition to partaking in these enforcement bands, they also frequently stage public demonstrations, criticizing the "shameless nakedness of women who trample on the blood of young men who gave their lives to the revolution and died a martyr's death" (320).

Many of the rationales given for imposition of hejab deal with women's perceived "natural" and inherent biological inferiority. Whereas men possess a "calm and orderly nature," women conversely possess an "unruly passion" (319). As a result, men are constantly in danger of becoming aroused by the "lasciviousness" of women who are always a temptation (Afshar 1998: 199). Veiling is seen as a means to protect women and their modesty. After all, the Koran (verse XXIV: 31) demands of women that they "cast down their looks and guard their private parts and do not display their ornaments, zinat" (198).

Women who are not veiled will become sex objects; they will end up like women in the West, who are undergoing terrible disasters of exploitation. In the West, women have been "forced to abandon their natural talents, as created by God and endorsed by men" (1991: 319). Instead they have been pushed into the workplace and, as a result, have been subjected to the awful demands of the double burden of both working for wages and undertaking all the reproductive labor. This situation causes damage to and is in direct opposition to their "gentle and sensitive nature." Not surprisingly, many of these same Western women have refused their "holy" duty of motherhood, resulting in an unloved generation of children who are lacking the tenderness and love of a mother and have in turn created a disrupted and alienated society (319). Thus veiling is also a means of expressing a national identity — one separate and unique from that of the West.

Ironically it was indeed solidarity and rejection of Western values which first prompted Iranian women to willingly take up the veil in the revolution of 1979. Prior to the revolution, Iran was undergoing a process of modernization under a corrupt monarchy supported by the United States. Women of the traditional segment of the middle class were threatened both by this modernization and the imposition of Western norms and values. Many were artisans, merchants, shopkeepers, and traders who could not compete with the surplus and cheap price of industrially produced goods. They also felt insulted by the Shah's proposed "new woman" who was expected to "ornament and show herself in order to please both the public and her husband, while at the same time serve as a cheap commodity in the labor force" (Tohidi 1991: 257). Veiling became a way to embrace traditional norms and to reject Westernization. In order to show solidarity, many university-educated, leftish, and middle-class women who had never worn the veil took in up during demonstrations and rallies against the perceived common enemy (252). Islamist women as well support the veil, believing it to be liberating because it allows them to effectively function in public society, freeing them from both harassment and questioning of their reputations as honorable and moral women (Afshar 1998: 200).

Feminist Critiques of Veiling: Interpretation of the Koran

Many feminists argue against the imposition of hejab. Most point to a problem of interpretation of the Koran. In addition, many women claim that the actual text of the Koran which deals with veiling (XXIII: 59) may only be addressed to the Prophet's wives and is not specific about what constitutes a veil.

> "O Prophet! Say to your wives and your daughters and women of the believers that they let down upon them their overgarment; this will be more proper, that they will be known and thus they will not be given trouble; and Allah is forgiving, merciful" (Afshar 1998: 13).

In addition, modesty is called for on the part of men as well as women. According to verse XXIV: 30 and 31, both should "cast down their looks and guard their private parts" (14). Verse XXIV: 31 seems reasonable enough as it states that women should not

> "display their ornaments except what appear thereof; they should draw their veils over their bosoms, and not display their beauty except to their husbands or their fathers ... and they should not stamp their feet in order to draw attention to their ornaments" (14).

This could be interpreted only that women cover their bosom and act chastely, as should men.

Feminists also argue that the veil as it is imposed is a distinctly misogynistic practice. It has become a barrier with the purpose of separating women both spatially and physically from men. In this way, women are not protected; they are only made into outcasts. By imposing the veil, men are demonstrating their lack of trust in their women relatives. Feminists contend that men are afraid of women's sexuality and thus wish to control women through silence and stillness (14). Other women argue that enforced veiling is an affront to their liberty and freedom (198).

Whichever the case may be, it is difficult to ignore the fact that the chador is an extremely debilitating and uncomfortable piece of clothing. As one woman surgeon says, "they just don't understand that you cannot perform surgery ... with a maghnae (a scarf which fits tightly under the chin) strangling your throat" (Esfandiari 1997: 134). Yet perhaps this is understood all too well. Since the revolution many public areas, including schools and universities are now sex-segregated. As a result, some girls' schools have had to close due to a shortage of teachers, and literacy rates are dropping. Women are also banned from studying in several fields, and married women are prohibited from attending public school entirely. The legal age for marriage has been lowered to nine years, and polygamy and temporary marriage (which can last anywhere from a few minutes to ninety-nine years) have been reinstated. Women have lost the right to abortion, the right to seek a divorce (except in extremely unusual circumstances), and the right to legally leave their homes without their husband's permission (Tohidi 1991: 253-254). In light of these concurrent policies, it is difficult to argue that the enforcement of hejab is anything but a means to control women's behavior and return them to the household and out of the public sphere altogether. "Through the dress code, the state endeavors to define and symbolically control the role of women" (Esfandiari 1997: 133).

Resistance to Veiling / Veiling as Resistance

Despite the use of force and intimidation to enforce observance of Islamic hejab, some women display resistance. One of the ways in which they do this is to push the limits of the dress code as far as they can. "By flaunting the dress code, women not only seek to score points against the authorities; they also strive to assert autonomy over their own persons" (133). Women are still required to cover their hair and wear robes which reach from neck to ankle in public, but in the wealthier section of northern Tehran raincoats and overcoats are now worn instead of robes. Robes come in a variety of colors and are becoming shorter in contemporary Iran. Many women have replaced the maghnae with flowing, loose scarves. Young girls around the campus of Tehran University have become especially famous. They wear colorful scarves which allow the tip of pony tails to slip free. They routinely flaunt their kakols, a fringe or bob of hair showing beneath their scarves, in front of revolutionary guards (133).

Many women also use the dress code to their advantage as a means to increase their mobility in society. For example, if a woman is seeking admittance to a university or a promotion at work, she will not exhibit the slightest resistance to the dress code. While in public, she will wear the correct low-heeled shoes, a dark scarf pulled over her forehead (completely covering her hairline), and the plainest outer garments she can find. She will also adhere to the most pious and politically correct way of behavior. She will not allow herself to be seen in public with men who are not close family members and will discourage male attention. She will also make sure to observe the fast and to pray. Because of her unquestionably pious behavior, she will be noticed and reported on as a moral, pious woman, and her chances for promotion or admission will increase. However, no one will know that "at home she is looking at American videos smuggled in from Kuwait" (Friedl 1994: 164). Using the hejab as a means to become educated and subtly altering the hejab are defined as two of women's key means of resistance in modern Iran (Esfandiari 1998: 135).

Egypt

Resurgence of Veiling

Unlike the situation of forced veiling in Iran, women in Egypt have voluntarily taken up the veil. In the early 1970s, Egyptian university students began veiling, and the trend soon spread to the lower-middle classes, with white-collar workers in the government and public sectors being the most visible group of muhaggabat (the veiled ones). The majority of younger women in most government offices were veiled by 1985 (Hoodfar 1997: 322).

In fact, veiling is now quite common among both university women and young professionals (Duval 1998: 61).

To the Western eye, this appeared quite shocking. After all, Egyptian women had begun to publically discard the veil in the 1920s in protest against "social and political marginalisation" (Fawzi El-Solh and Mabro 1994: 9). Unlike their grandmothers and mothers who had protested to ban mandatory veiling, however, modern Egyptian women did not adopt the milaya laff, or "enveloping sheet" (10). Rather they adopted a new type of Islamic dress consisting of a turban or scarf worn with a long, Western-style dress (El-Ziyy El-Islami). The head covering must conceal the hair and often also covers the shoulders. This is very different from the modes of dress and veiling displayed by the peasant (fela-heen) women or the more traditional urban lower classes (balady) and serves to "separate modern educated women from the traditional women whose style of dress carries the implication of 'backwardness' and lack of sophistication" (Hoodfar 1997: 322).

Several reasons were given by women for voluntary veiling. One common argument states that women's return to veiling is liberating. In doing so, women are choosing to reclaim their bodies and refusing to accept capitalism and consumerism and, as a result, will be delivered from the exploitation brought about by imperialists and colonizers, or the West (Gerami 1996: 86). Many women are indeed angry over the perceived loss of traditional values which has accompanied development and modernization. Thus the adoption of the veil can be seen as both a nationalistic and anti-Western protest. As in Iran, women are attempting to assert their cultural identity. "What they are actually protesting against is the vision of womanhood presented by the West, the image of the future imposed by modernization, and the inflation caused by economic dependency on other powers" (Duval 1998: 64-65). Veiling is also thought, as in Iran, to serve as a protection from harassment by men. As one woman says, "being totally covered saves me from the approaches of men and hungry looks. I feel more free, purer, and more respectable" (Duval 1998: 63). Yet, these arguments for veiling completely neglect the social factors going on at the time.

Feminist Critiques of Veiling: Social and Cultural Perspectives

Feminists often note that it is not surprising that the resurgence in veiling coincided with two social phenomena in

Egyptian culture: the rise in fundamentalism and the greater participation of women in the workplace. During the 1970s, fundamentalism was on the rise, and Islamic groups actively recruited and spread their word on college campuses. Because of their increasing activity, they were largely successful in appealing to large numbers of women, many from the lower and middle classes. Despite public counter-attacks on veiling by feminists, veiling continued to spread to the upper class (Badran 1991: 223). Feminists worried that women would begin to lose hard earned civil and human rights. Many saw the fundamentalists' and the government's strong urgence of women to take up the veil as a backslide; imposed seclusion, private abuse, and public persecution might follow. In addition, women might be forced to return to their traditional and "proper" place within the home and out of public life (Gerami 1996: 86).

Indeed, many critics of veiling point to the fact that the state began a propagation of an ideology which encouraged women to retreat into their homes and which aimed to curtail women's public life. Yet despite the state's lack of promotion of women's full employment, the migration of men to neighboring oil rich countries and rising inflation pushed more women into the workforce. As the men left, women were left behind to cope. Even though many purported to have taken up the veil in response to and in order to prevent male harassment, this is often criticized as "passive rather than active resistance to male intimidation" (Badran 1991: 224). After all, it is men who are doing the harassing; it should be their responsibility to control their own inappropriate behaviors. It is their creation of a threatening and hostile work environment, not women's so-called inherent seductive and disruptive nature, which is to blame.

Veiling is even more damaging and limiting to women, argue feminists, given that women's status in Egypt may already be on the decline. Legally, they are losing ground in terms of political rights and family protection; they may also be losing employment and educational opportunities. The same oil rich countries which drained men in the 1970s and 1980s are now experiencing depressions and oil glut, and this has eliminated many jobs for guest workers in addition to negatively impacting the local job market. Thus many returning and local workers have begun calling for women to return to the home in order to increase availability of jobs for men. Protective legislation which would give women mandatory part-time jobs, early retirement, or penalize men with working wives (through the denial of promotion, bonuses, pay insurance, and other measures) are also being considered and enacted (Gerami 1996: 87-88). Examining these circumstances adds weight to feminists' arguments; these measures are beginning to look remarkably similar to those proposed and enacted in Iran immediately after the revolution.

Veiling as Resistance

As in Iran, women use the veil as a means of resistance to culturally defined roles and expectation, seeking to negotiate their surroundings with the tools available to them. For example, one interpretation of veiling explains that women are "carving out legitimate public space for themselves" (Duval 1998: 61). By veiling, women are granted a legitimate excuse to be outside the home without the worry of questions directed at their reputations. After all, if they are veiled, they must be honorable and pious women; thus they must naturally have a good reason to be out late at night without an escort. Women are also using veiling as a tool to insert themselves into previously all-male domains such as mosques. This is demonstrated plainly in the experiences of one Egyptian woman who faced objection to her attendance at a lesson with a group of children in the main part of the mosque.

> "It was degrading and humiliating the way this man looked at me, as if I were nothing — a piece of garbage. He waved at me with his hands as if he was scaring off a little dog and ordered me to confine myself to the women's quarters which is very small and terribly hot now in summer. I thought to myself, I am wearing the Islamic dress, and am totally respectable in every way, so I just gave him my back and ignored him totally. I heard him mumbling in anger and then he went away. I think he learned a lesson he will never be able to forget" (62).

Arguably, freedom of mobility has increased; women are able to attend weddings and lessons with other women without the consents of male relatives (husbands, fathers, or brothers). Yet, women are gaining this mobility by using male standards. They are not granted respect due to acknowledgment of their status as equal human beings. Rather, they are marginalized; men, through their use of harassment, are defining the limits of acceptable behavior for women. In other words, even though the veil may be beneficial, it functions as a reminder that women are unwelcome in a male defined world, and in order to play a role in this world, they must play by the rules set down by men. They are an illness or pollutant which must be contained at all costs. As in Iran, women are a threat and thus their sexuality and conduct must be rigidly controlled through restrictions on clothing.

Another benefit of the veil is its ability to allow women to conserve their incomes. If they veil, they only need two or three outfits; there is no need to buy an excess of fashionable clothing (62-63). One example of this increase of mobility and conservation of income took place in the life of an Egyptian woman named Sommayya. She had recently finished her teacher training and was preparing to teach when her fiancé started to object to her having a career. Her mother and eldest sister supported his decision, pointing out that she would lose more money than she would make if she were to teach. She would be required to pay bus fares and be expected to eat lunch with her colleagues at work. In addition she would have to spend a large amount of money on clothes since it is considered not respectable for a teacher to work in cheap or old clothes. Finally people would talk about her reputation if she spent time on overcrowded buses with men of questionable morals. In order to solve her problem, Sommayya decided to take up the veil and requested that the Ministry of Education provide her a teaching appointment within walking distance of her house (her right as a married woman). This is remarkably similar to Iranian women's use of the veil to become educated or promoted.

> "I wear a long skirt and this scarf ... if I have only two sets of clothes I can look smart at all times because nobody expects muhaggabat (the veiled ones) to wear new clothes every day. This will save me a lot of money. It will also prevent people from talking about me, or questioning my honor or my husband's. In this way I have solved all the problems, and my husband's family are very happy that he is marrying a muhaggaba" (Hoodfar 1997: 323-324).

Yet, if women were not judged by a harsher standard of beauty than are men, this worry of being unfashionable would not be an issue.

Veiling also allows women to demand that their husbands recognize their Islamic rights. Husbands should not claim their wives wages as their own and are expected to fulfill their duty of providing for the family. In addition, many women take up the veil as protest when they marry and must move to neighborhoods on the outskirts of the city due to rising prices. In this circumstance, educated women wish to distinguish themselves from their lower class balady and falaheen neighbors. Thus they are able to separate themselves and still be considered to be neighborhood members of good standing (234-235).

The United States
Holdeman Mennonites and A Return to Modesty

In the United States, veiling is not widespread and usually occurs only in ethnic communities of orthodox Jewish or Muslim women. It is still possible, however, to liken veiling to issues of dress and control in this country. One of the most obvious examples occurs in the communities of Holdeman Mennonites. Another, arguably more disturbing, example is currently taking place in popular culture. The rise of the Religious Right and the main streaming of Christian fundamentalism has brought to the forefront the backlash against the feminist movement of the 1970s. Not surprisingly, a new book written by Wendy Shalit, entitled A Return to Modesty: Discovering the Lost Virtue, which calls upon women to dress more modestly and even consider veiling, has become wildly popular.

A Return to Modesty calls secular women to take up the veil and/or modest dress. After all, it protects women from both harassment and rape and is well suited to their natural sensitive temperament (Shalit 1999: 117). In addition, modesty is biologically inherent to women, despite American society's assaults on it, an argument comparable to that in Iran regarding women's natural sensitive temperament (118). According to Shalit, men should behave modestly as well, but there is a catch. Men are not naturally modest and biologically need sex more than women. Thus, it is women's responsibility to act as role models to men and to function as the gatekeepers to sexual relations, and, in doing so, transform society.

> "If all girls suddenly announced they would not sleep with boys until they quit the gangs and gave them engagement rings, society could very well change overnight, but if the boys made a similar announcement about the girls, everybody would probably burst out laughing" (149).

This sort of logic sounds almost exactly like the logic used to enforce the veil in Iran as well as sounding remarkably similar to women's proposed justification for voluntary veiling in Egypt. It also sounds eerily like the type of logic used to discredit and blame victims of rape and sexual harassment who displayed that "they wanted it" by their seductive dress. What is most disturbing, however is that this book was in its sixth printing and received rave reviews after only one year.

An example of established modesty in the United States lies in the beliefs and practices of Holdeman Mennonites, who can trace their roots to small numbers of Mennonites who immigrated first to Pennsylvania in the eighteenth century. In search of religious freedom and branded as heretics, many immigrated from Germany and Switzerland to Holland and Russia and then on to North America. Linked to a radical group known as Anabaptists who first appeared during the Protestant Reformation of the sixteenth century, they believe foremost in separating themselves as much as possible from the world. They take this belief from Romans 12:2, "Do not be conformed to this world, but be transformed by the renewal of your mind, that you may prove what is the will of God, what is good and acceptable and perfect." One of the ways this is accomplished is through observance of plain dress (Graybill and Arthur 1999: 13).

Within the Mennonite religious community there are different standards for the sexes when it comes to dress. Men generally dress in jeans and plaid shirts, a style which allows them to pass quite easily in the outside world. Women's dress, however, has remained relatively unchanged since the nineteenth century (17). Thus they are easily identifiable in society, as are veiled women in Egypt and Iran. Girls and women are expected to wear shirtwaist dresses with long, wide skirts and a fitted bodice which buttons down the center to the waist (Arthur 1993: 72). Most important to a woman's dress is her head covering. It must be black, cover her hair (which remains always uncut), and be pinned to a bun. Jewelry and cosmetics are prohibited. Even though Mennonites believe that all clothing should be scrutinized according to perceived New Testament standards, and though not enforced through the use of violence like the hejab is in Iran or by sexual harassment as in Egypt, it is only women who are subjected to this scrutiny (Graybill and Arthur 1999: 17).

All of the ministers and deacons in the church are men, as in Iran, and they are responsible for monitoring the community members' behavior and women's dress. Mennonite's are supposed to exercise self-denial, and this should take a visible form through appearance. Women are expected to be thin and "sober in demeanor and appearance" (Arthur 1993: 73). The most visible symbol of a woman's self-denial is her head covering, which represents her submission to her husband and to God (Graybill and Arthur 1999: 18). Due to such strict norms, it is not difficult to be labeled as deviant, and the most common offenses deal with clothing. Once so labeled, women face continuous surveillance and the threat of expulsion. Most often reproval is handled solely by the ministers, but sometimes the offender is brought in front of the entire congregation. If one is expelled, she faces shunning. She is not allowed to eat at the same table as the family or to have economic or social contact or interactions with any member of the community.

In addition, women monitor each other's behavior out of "Christian love" (Arthur 1993: 75). If a woman commits a transgression, she can expect it to be the topic of conversation among her friends; they will also confront her directly, expressing concern for her spirituality. Again, clothing is most often the issue. "Members are continually aware of clothing and use it to gauge a person's submission of self to the group" (75). Thus, as in Iran and Egypt, a woman's clothing is the most substantial measurement of her piety and respectability.

Feminist Theoretical Objections: Social Control and The Pedagogy of Shame

As is a common theme in contexts with dress restrictions, other behavior is restricted as well. Not surprisingly, some feminists note, this restricted behavior usually falls into the category of any type of behavior which would grant women power or autonomy. For example, Conservative Mennonite groups traditionally oppose higher education; it is unnecessary and un-Christian. Rarely is earning a college degree acceptable, and even then it must be approved by the ministers. Having knowledge is considered to be synonymous with pridefulness. Desiring too much knowledge would inspire too much abstract thought and, consequently, dissent.

In one instance, a young woman enrolled in a junior college outreach program near her home. Since she was a child she had wanted to be a doctor. She had made this aspiration known, and many other members had previously encouraged her to become a vocational nurse instead. The church ministers in her community, however, publically censured her and ordered her to quit school. During her interrogation at a public hearing, she was accused of either having mental problems or of being a lesbian. As a result, she was kept under close scrutiny for several years until she eventually married and conceived several children (Graybill and Arthur 1999: 19).

In the Mennonite faith, sexual desire is strictly controlled as well, as it threatens the spiritual nature. Though in theory both men and women are responsible for monitoring sexual urges, the vast majority of the burden falls to the women (20). Women are judged according to the effect their sexuality has on men, especially ministers, and ministers do not see the contradiction inherent in this type of logic (24). This sounds familiar; neither the ministers in Iran nor the men in Egypt do, either. Consequently, tightening controls on girls' clothing occur just as they reach adolescence, the age where attracting a prospective husband becomes the main concern and their bodies are beginning to develop (22). Women and men are kept separate from each other beginning at adolescence. For example, they sit on separate sides in church and may only date with a chaperone present. They are also not allowed to be alone together until married. Birth control is prohibited, and adulthood is synonymous with motherhood. This is spelled out in classes segregated by sex in which members learn church dictates of acceptable sexual behavior. Public displays of affection are discouraged, and the actual sex act is to be "accomplished quickly and efficiently, with no time wasted on foreplay" (20). Clearly, controlling women's dress, and thus their sexuality, forms a sort of social control which functions to keep them in subordinate positions in the Mennonite community, as it does in Egypt and Iran.

Though the majority of American women do not veil, a phenomenon observed in mainstream American culture arguably functions as a corollary to veiling. According to many feminists, women are subjected to a discourse of shaming present in institutions and everyday interactions, in effect, constituting a "pedagogy of shame" much like the one experienced by women in Iran and Egypt through the rigid control of dress (Bartky 1996: 225). It is a pervasive feature of American life, and women internalize these messages of inferiority and guilt. As a result, women are more shame-prone than men, as shame is defined as "a pervasive sense of personal inadequacy" (226).

Feminists point to evidence in the form of women's "veiled" behavior. Women are documented to have lower self-esteem than men, be less assertive, have less overall confidence, and poorer self-concepts (229). In mixed discussions, both in and out of the classroom, women are noticeably quieter and often speak in a phenomenon termed "women's language." Their speech is marked by false starts and hesitations; comments are introduced by self-denigrated expressions. In addition, declarative sentences are often stated in a questioning intonation, turning them into requests for affirmation or help, and "tag" questions such as "isn't it?" are placed at the end of statements. This method of talking effectively damages the speaker's effectiveness and credibility (230). It also allows men to dominate linguistic space, and is clearly related to their dominance of physical space, and thus their dominant role in society. Though women are not physically veiled, they have been pushed into subordinate positions through other means. Thus, donning veils would diminish their status further; veiling American women would only be acknowledging the "invisible veil" which already exists.

Resistance and Self-Authorizing

As in Iran and Egypt, women use the tools available to them to negotiate their surroundings. Though not visible like the alteration of hejab, women's language, while an example of subjugation, can also be seen as a means of self-authorization. After all, women are still speaking, and by using this form of speech they are able to signal that they are acknowledging their own inadequacy before anyone else can, while still expressing their views. Some Mennonite women, similar to Egyptian and Iranian women, use their clothing as a means of negotiation and resistance. This is most obvious is younger women but is exercised by women of all ages.

Adolescence is recognized by the community as a rough period, and men usually defer the raising of daughters to their wives during this time. Girls may secretly wear "worldly" clothing by hiding it in lockers at school and changing before returning home. As one young girl states,

"I kept some worldly things at school. I also wore two-inch-wide belts, so that when I rolled up the waistband to shorten the skirt, the roll wouldn't show. This way, dresses could be long around adults and short at school like the other [non-Mennonite] girls" (Arthur 1993: 78).

Even though cosmetics are prohibited by the community, it is not unusual for girls to wear minimal makeup and foundation, subtle enough so that it is not noticeable by the ministers. Young women are also granted slightly more freedom with their clothing, though this is carefully monitored. Many spend much time determining how to alter structural details of dresses to make them more attractive, often adding pleats, yokes, and tucks. In addition, applied details are overlooked if they are considered to be functional (79).

Women who are married and have born children are expected to become more submissive and display greater conformity to the dress code, yet deviations do occur. For example, shoes are supposed to be black or brown with heels no smaller than a dime, and no open toes or heels are allowed. However, many Mennonite women wish to appear taller since they are short. Thus when three-inch-wedge-heeled shoes became fashionable in the 1970s, they became quite popular with the women. "The ministers complained that these were too worldly, but what could they do? We'd found the perfect solution to get around the rules!" (79). In addition, at a period when brown and black shoes went out of style and became hard to find, women had to use shoe dye to adapt lighter colored shoes. Due to the unreliability of the dye and the variation in material, many shoes came out slightly different shades such as mauve. This added some color to women's wardrobes, and even though the ministers complained, the shoes were considered acceptable since to throw them out would be wasteful (79).

In another ingenious twist, Holdeman Mennonite women altered the construction of their garments. Traditionally, dresses are supposed to fasten with buttons down the front, but this takes extra time both to make the garments and to get dressed. Women could not convince the ministers to allow them to replace the buttons with zippers, but they did persuade the ministers to allow them to sew zippers into the sides of dresses to make getting dressed easier. In addition, polyester knit fabrics were adopted rapidly as they became available; they make sewing dresses quicker and easier, and they do not require ironing. Women were careful to stick with fabrics, which closely resembles traditional cotton calico prints, however. This subtle alteration of dresses by Mennonite women seems very similar to the alterations made to the hejab by Iranian women. Finally, in recent years, a segment of Mennonite women have been exhibiting noticeable weight gain, which can be interpreted as a resistance to the ideal thin woman (80).

Conclusion: Does Modesty Protect Women?

Clearly the context for veiling and modest dress are vastly different in all three of these cultures: Iran is forced, Egypt is voluntary, and the United States varies between required and suggested depending on the community involved. However, the arguments put forth sound quite similar. Whether it is the women themselves, the Christian Right, or the Islamic Fundamentalists, all agree that restricting women's dress will protect them from the harassment of men. The logic behind this argument is the same in all cases; women are naturally tempting and seductive, and men are unable to control their own sexual urges and behavior. It is ironic, to say the least, that it is never put forth to men that they are responsible for their own behavior; even though, it is indeed men who are doing the harassing. After all, if they are naturally more clear-headed, wise, and rational, it should stand to reason that they would be able to monitor their own actions effectively. It is all too clear, however, that restricting women's dress is a method of controlling other aspects of their lives and keeping them in subordinate positions. Even though women through their resourcefulness may find ways to use it to their advantage, modesty does not protect women. Rather, it maintains a world of hostility and shame directed towards women and thus a world of male privilege, dominance, and power.

References

Afshar, Haleh. 1997. Women, Marriage and the State in Iran. In
The Women, Gender & Development Reader, ed. Nalini
Visvanathan et al., 317-320. London: Zed Books.

_____. 1998. Islam and Feminisms: An Iranian Case-Study.
London: Macmillan Press.

Arthur, Linda Boynton. 1993. Clothing, Control, and Women's
Agency: The Mitigation of Patriarchal Power. In Negotiating
at the Margins: The Gendered Discourses of Power and
Resistance, ed. Sue Fisher and Kathy Davis, 66-84. New
Brunswick: Rutgers University Press.

Badran, Margot. 1991. Competing Agendas: Feminists, Islam and
the State in 19th and 20th Century Egypt. In Women, Islam
and the State, ed. Deniz Kandiyoti, 201-236. Philadelphia:
Temple University Press.

Bartky, Sandra Lee. 1996. The Pedagogy of Shame. In Feminisms
and Pedagogies of Everyday Life, ed. Carmen Luke, 225-
241. Albany: State University of New York Press.

Duval, Soroya. 1998. New Veils and New Voices: Islamist

    Women's Groups in Egypt. In Women and Islamization:

    Contemporary Dimensions of Discourse on Gender

    Relations, eds. Karin Ask and Marit Tjomsland, 45-72.

    Oxford: Berg.

Esfandiari, Haleh. 1997. Reconstructed Lives: Women & Iran's

    Islamic Revolution. Washington, D.C.: The Woodrow

    Wilson Center Press.

Fawzi El-Solh, Camilla and Judy Mabro. 1994. Introduction: Islam

    and Muslim Women. In their Muslim Women's Choices:

    Religious Belief and Social Reality, 1-32. Oxford: Berg.

Friedl, Erika. 1994. Sources of Female Power in Iran. In In the Eye

    of the Storm: Women in Post-revolutionary Iran, ed. Mahnaz

    Afkhami and Erika Friedl, 151-167. Syracuse: Syracuse

    University Press.

Gerami, Shahin. 1996. Women and Fundamentalism: Islam and Christianity. New York: Garland Publishing, Inc. Graybill, Beth and Linda B. Arthur. 1999. The Social Control of Women's Bodies in Two Mennonite Communities. In Religion, Dress, and the Body, ed. Linda B. Arthur, 9-29. Oxford: Berg.

Hoodfar, Homa. 1997. Return to the Veil: Personal Strategy and Public Participation in Egypt. In The Women, Gender & Development Reader, ed. Nalini Visvanathan et al., 320-325. London: Zed Books.

Shalit, Wendy. 1999. A Return to Modesty: Discovering the Lost Virtue. New York: Touchstone.

Tohidi, Nayereh. 1991. Gender and Islamic Fundamentalism: Feminist Politics in Iran. In Third World Women and the Politics of Feminism, ed. Chandra Talpade Mohanty, Ann Russo, and Lourdes Torres, 251-267. Bloomington: Indiana University Press.

www.ingramcontent.com/pod-product-compliance
Lightning Source LLC
Chambersburg PA
CBHW070523290526
45790CB00003B/1275